SOJOURN ON A RIVER

SOJOURN ON A RIVER

TERRY YATES

Pennington Press

SOJOURN ON A RIVER

TERRY YATES

CONTENTS

FOREWORD

I was fortunate to have had Terry Yates in my creative writing classes back when Jefferson Community College was part of the University of Kentucky. It did not take me very long to recognize in this young man was a fine talent, one I hoped I would have the opportunity sometime to write a foreword to a book of poetry of his. I am delighted that such an opportunity has now come my way.

Terry Yates is bright, he is original, he works just enough over the edge to create new and exciting images, fresh lines, and unusual thoughts that make the reader blink and respond, "Say What!" He has a sense of humor that often causes a person to twist all the way around and flip over backwards. But don't underestimate Terry's seriousness. Humor is just one of the ways he captures our thoughts. Complicated alloy tools, after all, were at first look, just smoky, runny metal; often the runniest and most smoky stuff becomes the hardest and sharpest steel.

Sojourn on a River is filled with short poems that'll make you smile and dance, songs that'll get you singing, and longer poems that put new rafters in that circular building that sits on your shoulders.

You're going to recognize right off Terry's impressive wit, which is soft as a feather but strong as a tire iron. Wit plays a major part in all his thoughts and images. In fact, I'd say wit is the main course in this six course meal you're about to enjoy. Once you get the hang of it, you're in for a real gourmet treat.

As you read his work, expect the unexpected (a sign of good poetry by the way). In many ways, it's the old magician's trick: while we focus on the unimportant hand, the other hand explodes the magical wonder.

Consider, for example, his short poem "Notches in a Six Gun Sleep" which goes like this:

I dreamt a Dali Western
Where I was the guy
Wearing a Picasso
style sombrero
under a separate sky
Snake bite.

Strange wonderful images throughout, but that "snake bite" is the final unexpected notch in this six gun sleep.

You can open this book at any page and immediately be rewarded by what you read. You'll recognize a theme by the time you finish, but each poem is an island within itself and there's plenty of exploring to do.

This is the kind of writing you'll want to savor. Read it slowly, one poem at a time--not the whole book all at once. Remember you don't want to try to swallow everything at once. Relax. Savor it. It's not often you have an opportunity for such epicurean delight on an author's first book. This is one of those times. Enjoy.

--Lee Pennington,
Louisville, KY - July, 2020

THE DISTANCE BETWEEN
HEAVEN AND EARTH

The speed of light is 186,000 miles per second
The speed of Spirit cannot be clocked.

THE UNKNOWN TERROR

The Monster: Bloodshot eyes, in need
Of dental work, very bad temperament

The Mob: Terperamental needlework
Growing sharp teeth, smell of blood

The Shivers: What no amount of bandages
can cover

ATOMS AT PLAY

The many gnats in the summer air
Assemble, disassemble and reassemble
Isn't that what they say the universe
Is doing?

Out of the Metro   Jill Baker 2020

OUT OF THE METRO

Sliding doors splash a toe to toe dash
Zigzag hashtag people frozen pop up
even now to up elevator
meat locker heaven help us
turnstile click Mississippi click
Mississippi click miss step semi click stuck
seeing the result of sunshine
next in line
Uber Cell Batt Dead

SHUTTER LIGHT

Flicker rich candlelight eyes
view the magic show in wonder
Cotton Eye Candy
one eye being lazy
Two Eyes were the Other

NOTCH IN A SIX GUN SLEEP

I dreamt a Dali Western
Where I was the guy
Wearing a Picasso
style sombrero
under a separate sky
Snake bite

PASSING INTO THE FUTURE

From rotary wall phones
and vacuum tubes
to all you
care to desire
in any venue

THE FUNNY PAGES

Yesterday can only be fact
Tomorrow can only be fiction
Both may be contradictions

THE LITTLE RED METAL TOOLBOX

I told sons (when they were
years apart) when it seemed the
right median age to say
what I was to say:

"In Life you will need
a little red toolbox if you wish to succeed
Inside you will find
A bent rusty Philips screwdriver
And a flashlight without batteries."

They looked at each other
brother to brother
and asked what
does that mean?

I answered:
You're on your own kid.
Life will throw you curves

and so many verbs and we won
the war against the British
that is the sum of my wisdom
for a very good reason this night

They fell asleep minutes after
I left the room.

BASED ON A PAINTING

Autumn house
On summer beach
bleached white from
elements, time and obvious
neglect
Yet buckets of roses
line the rickety porch
Theatrical red against
dull care
Waves crash
Sand dunes curl
Picket fence disheveled
Roof so care worn
Windows with speckles
of sea and Sunday
Front door slightly open
Footprints fresh in the sand

GEEZER ONE AND FIFTYNINE

When I was a kid rotary phones were standard
Wall phones were the wave of the future
In my late teens push tone phones came out
These days everything that can be imagined
Flies off the shelf with rapid abandon
I would like a day where all things
remain as they are for at least the time
it takes to sit on the porch

ARSENIC ELEGY

There is arsenic in all things poignant
As surely as poison in nature has degrees
making some leaves a bother
others simply in the breeze
of pause in an elegy
briefly touching a rose

HERO OF THE PARADIGM

There say the right colors
all salted lemon lime
like a silver tongued devil
hero of the paradigm
The states of grace
are altered in time
hear the conquered
singing in rhyme

Flow charts mean nothing
Because nothing is flawed
examined to the tooth
in long books of law
The paradigm is as
short as it's long
pleasing to the ear
a young blood's song

Existence is useless

without common cause
voices linger in
the common walls
Magic in manner
and in deed seem just
Remember ancient writers
in dreams if you must

Overblown, overboard
eventually convicted
of many crimes
now all admitted
Clowns stretch paradigm
to the very limit
After hours in sleep
history never quits it

The spider is dead
the spider has died
things still get trapped
to the web from inside
When the paradigm shifts
many will follow
into the vast lands
of many sleepy hollers.

Marble Hill   Jill Baker

MARBLE HILL AND THE
PADDLEWHEEL ALLIANCE

I was in a protest march
yes I was
in the nineteen seventies
late in the decade
I believe it seemed
like March

The object of the protest
was Marble Hill
a nuclear power plant
that if God forbid an accident
the Ohio Valley
would guarantee
a disaster unto me

This will not stand

When the march with all
the homemade signs

and sheets
reached the City Hall
We all fell to the concrete
just like we were dead
on account of radiation

I remember a lady of some years
walking over the lame of us
cursing from top to bottomus
the lot of us
protesters with signs and little else

That day in Indiana could have
maybe helped stop a thing not to be
brought about maybe forever

I was young in my teens
I followed my best ideals
like four kings
Plus it was fun.

THE GHOST OF JOHN BROWN

Before his execution
John Brown said:
The sins of this land
will be paid with blood.

I'll ask his ghost
Is this blood enough?

Blood of everyone
spilled in such
uselessness

Is the tinder packed
with the "right" people
to burn in the service
of all that is evil,

John Brown Justice
in a Quick needs a sharp

dagger.

We all bleed
Monsters gather on Main Street
The reward of Cruelty
is blood without end.

John Brown pitched a rock
in the gears,
stopping time for
many years.

SET OF SEVEN SONGS

I MIGHT BE FREE

I might be free
to think out loud
to state an opinion
and stand by it proud,
to pontificate
the day away
I might be free
Someone says...no way.

I might be free
all over the place
to make my mark
in the human race
to be all I seem
no matter what they say
I might be free
Someone says...no way.

I might be free

according to the rule
I overheard
outside the vestibule
The Romans weren't Italian
and the Greeks have feet of clay
I might be free
Someone says...no way.

I might be free
to ramble on
about the care and maintenance
of Spanish unicorns
just before Pegasus
flies away
I might be free
Someone says...no way.

[Harmonica break]
I might be free
to follow the trail
that gets out of
my imaginary jail
I'll be on the run
from Guantanamo Bay
I might be free
Someone says...no way.

I might be free
up until the end
when I spend my
very last dividend
We'll have to see,
It's hard to tell

I might be free
Someone says...Go to Hell.

[Harmonica
Break: spoken word: You just can't catch a break man.
Harmonica Out]

SAVING FACEBOOK
BLUES.COM

I wasn't known by the company I keep
Cause I wasn't on Facebook with people to seek
I logged on just one time
three weeks later I was still on line...
Lots of people in there...
Minds all buzzing
Somewhat...
Like real life.

I was friended by many ladies from London
Who were all tired, divorced, broke and...a...lonesome
I said, "I got troubles to the bone, please just
leave me alone. I said DELETE...
My troubles are all in my head.

A funny thing happened on the way to the forum
I got losted and clicked onto a foursome...
You shouldn't invade people's lives

and I should be thinking of my wife...
...but what the hell...
I'm all about anonymous.

An identity thief doesn't have to sneak in the night
There is no time like a second ago to steal your life
They can pick your pockets without sleight of hand
three clicks and four more on demand...
It happens every three and half middle minutes...
Translated means...just now...
Nine million seven and twenty-nine on Sunday.

You can be stuck down in a deep dark cave
and still log onto the pages you save
Page up page down
You can slum it
or take it Downtown...
I got a million friends...
None I know so well...

Shakespeare said, "In all things be pithy"
but on Facebook it can be such a pity
You can't understand some people's meaning
some people are plain mean I'm just saying...
A Bitcoin for your thoughts...
...That's what I thought

You may find a long lost love
It may be dangerous
you may get twice a shove...
...all the way down the staircase...
You don't need to worry...

It's not possible to get hurt...
It's not actual...
It's all virtual...

Some people have outrageous theories
They believe what they say and believe
it dearly...
They're not likely to be right
but then again Peter Pan may
fly by night...
I am exactly neutral... nutcase

Having friends doesn't mean you're not lonely
twenty new a minute asking for money
Every day is Halloween
there are some things that can't be unseen
That was messed up... if the truth be told.

The trash can is filled, the recycle bin is stolen
my fingers are numb and my eyes are swollen
Quite lucky to be alive...
at this moment
Cyber wise Godfrey Daniels!
I'm late...

All across this whole world wide
there is not a single solitary place where
you may ever find that you may one day
possibly hide...

They'll find you
you can find yourself

change your mind
be someone else...

My portrait don't look a thing
like me...

WAYWARD HILL

In a distant place during another time
Love was a passion
like a Red Blood Shine
A kind of Magic that worked its will
We took all the wrong turns
going up Wayward Hill

In the time of the present
the place don't look the same
I have reason to believe
the trees have been rearranged
Like a spell that's broken by taking a pill
at the Visitor's Center
up on Wayward Hill

The shelf life of love
should be measured in years
A mutual surrender
to each other's fears

Like a Voodoo doll
stays perfectly still
You can buy at the gift shop
Up on Wayward Hill

Into the far future
You can see on a clear day
Chasing the wind
After the dust has been swept away
The climb is the Thing
that tests your every skill
the path from The Pinnacle
takes you down
Wayward Hill.

DON'T TARRY ME

You can call me a charlatan
Liar and thief
Repeat it all night
with a sense of relief
I hear your voice
like an echo in reverse
and it sounds just like
a southern curse
On the hot tin roof
of the House of Mendacity
I can dance all summer day long
Don't tarry me

I'm on pins and needles
like in the electric chair
I'm not even sure
if I'm self aware
One thing is for certain
you're not on my mind

I can rest in peace
like it's gravy time
I hung my sugar canes
From a hickory tree
They sparkle with touch
Don't tarry me

Like the Frankenstein Monster
who's showing his age
I'm glad I have
triple A
I seldom speak
sometimes I'm blind
I'm stitched together
I'm five of a kind
I'm out in the countryside
and roaming free
I need a jump 'round midnight
Don't tarry me.

Of all my memories
I can only take one in three
There are some that seem
to trouble me
Put them in a box
Put them out on display
Count them down
till they all go away
On the Ides of March
I'll have something up my sleeve
I've crossed the Rubicon
Don't tarry me

You make me crazy
You always have
Crazy as a Hatter
and twice as mad
I went down the rabbit hole
forty days and nights
There wasn't enough time
to see all the sights
The pies on the table
all say "EAT ME"
I love my Wonder bread
Don't tarry me

I lost my train of thought
in the baggage car
She said "Don't show your face
They know who you are"
Feel like an imposter
on a faceless Halloween
meeting invisible people
like a go-between
I use an alias
like others say please
I'm never on time
Don't tarry me

Old as the hills
young as sawdust
If memory serves
we do as we must
You say our love
was a temporary need
That I'm a stranger now

who is lost in the weeds
I'm a fugitive on the run
from the eye that always sees
as I cross myself
Don't tarry me

Where did I stumble?
When did I falter?
Was it outside of church
or up near the altar?
A crime of passion
cannot be excused
Love is a distraction
and beauty is a ruse
Twist my arm
you'll get a guilty plea
It's all foreshadowed
Don't tarry me

The lady vanishes
into thin air
Feels like a game
of Truth or Dare
Sometimes she winks
She may even smile
all you got to do
is wait all the while
A broken heart
stays broken indeed
Romeo said to Juliet
"Don't tarry me"

Angels in the outfield

Chain gangs in the heat
The boxer needs a cutterman
The crowd's in disbelief
To make shadow and light
all disappear
is the sole business
Corinthians of the lone puppeteer
Art for art's sake
And veins that bleed
to great affect
Don't tarry me

The Mad Scientist throws his switches
way up on the hill
Uses unnatural selection
Looking for the triumph of the will
The Bishop reads Corintians
The townspeople are in a trance
I make my unlikely escape
by happenstance
I'm back on the road
dodging chicanery
roll up the window
Don't tarry me

The fire in the furnace
is hotter than hell
Nobody listens
everybody yells
In a time of reason
such things aren't condoned
In a time of madness
we are all accident prone

The more political the speech
the greater the trickery
I'm listening to Bob Dylan
Don't tarry me

Like a floating butterfly
circling above tea leaves
The world is in its Seventh Heaven
by the feel of the breeze
Life is short
and the days are long
Everybody shuffling
to the very same song
In a stir of events
there is great mystery
The Wizard is n the wind
Don't tarry me

I WISH I HAD YOUR COOL

I wish I had your cool
Seventy two degrees like it's all shade
Electric in the breeze
Strawberry Blond for a day
You got your cool on
And you get it on
Right away

I wish I had your cool
Raven on barbwire in the mist
No flinch or flutter
A persuasion I can't resist
You got your cool on
And you know
It's hard to miss

I wish I had your cool
You're a female Steve McQueen
In that Mustang Fastback

Burning Hi-Test gasoline
You got your cool on
And when it's on
All the lights are green

I wish I had your cool
Venus De Milo with the antidote
Rikki Lee is down the stairs
Singing about a lover's note
You got your cool on
And while it's on
That's all she wrote

I wish I had your cool
Mother may I under the circumstance
Over a friendly game of pool
Truth or consequence
You got your cool on
And when it's on
Ain't no game of chance

I wish I had your cool
Bobby Dylan bohemian style
In a court of many fools
You're a mosaic of many colored tiles
You got your cool on
And since it's been on
We are reconciled

ZOMBIE CATHOUSE WOMAN

My zombie cathouse woman
me and her are just fine
My zombie cathouse woman
me and her are just...fine
I lost one eye
and she is partially blind

She died in my arms
and I died in hers
She died in my arms
and I died in hers
We had the very same affliction
she was my Mercy Nurse

Scratch my back baby
catch is as catch can
Scratch my back now baby
catch is as catch can

What I got you can get
and I can call you my friend

Out among the living dead
but we are not dropping just yet
Chilling with the living dead
we are not dropping just yet
What I did in life
as a zombie I don't regret

Body snatchers in the cathouse
shaking down the nervous
The body snatchers in the cathouse
shaking down the nervous
Anybody could be John Dillinger
Anybody could be Melvin Pervis

She's a helcat zombie
when her hair is unfurled
One helcat kind of zombie
when her hair is unfurled
She docs the Zombie Cathouse Strut
and her toes are always curled

We took a sip of the cure
and threw the rest down the drain
Just one sip of the cure
threw the rest down the drain
I hate bad medicine
want to eat some rice and brains

My zombie cathouse woman

in her black and white way
My zombie cathouse woman
in her black and white way
She says the moon tonight is colorful
Honey let's make hay.

Sojourn on a River   Jill Baker

SOJOURN ON A RIVER

Oh mercy me
can't you tell
all things in a hand basket
gone to hell
At lightning speed
like the snap of a bow
life is worth living
over the rainbow

A simple truth
can become a dirty lie
but God's in his Heaven
by and by
Life is not a crime
it's a test
and soul seekers gather
in the wilderness

Shangri-La

in the piney wood
Love is for lovers
it's understood
What can be worse
than a broken heart
every breath you take
is a work of art

He said, "Welcome to my house,
step right in
Pull up a chair
my long lost friend."
There is safety in numbers
and here numbers overflow
now that you realize
life comes and goes.

Slouching toward Bethlehem
with sand in your shoes
For the very first time
you have nothing to lose
In the acreage of space
there's more than twenty mules
and time passes swiftly
right on schedule
Sojourn on a river
like Huckleberry Finn
Meeting strangers often
and some companions
The onion is ever peeled
forever more
and the stars will be shining
on that distant shore.

THE LIST MINUS WORDS

One: Words should not be necessary
Two: Use any mute
Three: Muted words will be used against you
Four: The full extent of the law will be speechless
Five: No real names given to those to blame
Coda: History

CRAZY EYE SAW

Teeth jigsaw as
Skeleton keys
To rooms abandoned
With dusty cotton
Dividers
As Jericho walls
A night to remember
Slipknot
And
Shoelace

TRAP DOOR

If not heaven sent
Expect the next
Two levels dark

See me Gone Away   Jill Baker

SEE ME GONE AWAY

I think when you are gone
From a thing it is just over
Goodbye to friends made
By coming this way
Lose a job
Move along cowboy

LIFEBOAT

Those among the survivors
who had money as if capital
could save a life
complained the most

THE DELUDED AND THE DISMAYED

The Deluded all say
Feed me more

The Dismayed all say
What are you saying?

Both get taken

THE MISFITS HAVE STRING THEORY

They know because
They see
All the ways
To trip
In all notions
Up and tangled

IF THERE WERE NO COLOR RED

Blue and purple would not be seen
In anything but a dream
Bent as such light would
Linger less in shadow

BANDWIDTH

Brinstorm in fine tune
With a squiggle wobble
Spectrum jigging off the shelf
Sounds from all the best grey matter
Seeming as Nashville radio
Signals

LUCK OF IRIS

With green
Disappeared
Into air
Soon after
Afternoon
A sense of medicine
For no less a swoon
Garden gloves
Pitched
as per
Procedure

ETHNO STATE

It seems we are made to
Hate each other
For vague reasons
That cost
Too many
Too much
In return
For not about
Nothing

Stupid Poets   Jill Baker

STUPID POETS LEAVE LOVE LETTERS

Pouring syrup onto cupcakes
Adding powdered sugar
Glitter and little sparkle things
Cut into tiny bites of paper
Lost to the furniture
Many years later found
Undated

POEMS COMIC BOOK STYLE

A book of poetry
Should be read similar
To a comic book
Comics have brief text
To image ratio
Poems and comics
Are wildly creative
Six panels per page plus
A skydiver trailing smoke
Like it's all over
Into the middle of the story
Without a beginning
And certainly
Without end

LUNA HALF SAIL

When shows are falling
Visible light
Is put to shame
By the sideshow Luna

HEAVEN WAITS FOR A BODY

A body left the celestial poker game
For another try at life on Earth
A sixth player is needed
To finish the hand

Hitchcock and the Blondes   Jill Baker

HITCHCOCK AND THE BLONDES

Beauty ablaze Technicolor California
The hair and its wave classic ice
Warmed by amber and light
with the edited shadows
The girl on the gallows
None of it credible
without the end credit
Wardrobe by Edith Head

LIFE AS OPEN BOOK

The age thumbed
May be your fate
With index
To judge
Glossary
Misleading

FIRST IMPRESSION

When the artist is compelled
To explain
All private notions
dissolve

GOLD IN THE VAN GOGH FIELDS

Concentric swirls among yellow
Hayfields leading to the
Church at Arles
Just passed the
Garden of St. Paul's Asylum
To the simple room
With the simple chair
Seeing the cigarette skull
Self portrait with Bandaged Ear
Even Gaugin saw madness
Explode in episodes
With no one to blame
Save the blue flame
Lilacs, iris and poppy
Hollyhocks and the sower's memory
Sorry never still life
Paint to the busy easel
Thanks for all the help, Theo

SECOND SET OF SEVEN SONGS

DELIA YA DEAL ME DIRTY

I'm exhausted and overwhelmed
could be melancholy too
All the stress of the world
and what they lead us to do
Delia ya deal me dirty
ever time or two

I could be the toast of Broadway
high up in the cash
You'd burn my toast every morning
until it's nearly ash
Delia ya deal me dirty
like a Mason jar smash

If your house was on fire
and you couldn't pay the rent
And I saved everything quick
down to the last red cent
Dealia ya deal me dirty

like the devil Heaven sent

We had a summer house
in the Isle of Mind
I remember the neighbors
like they are friends of mine
Delia ya deal me dirty
What makes you so unkind?

Delia is a woman
everybody knows
She'll break your heart
just to spite your nose
Delia ya deal me dirty
like a second hand rose

Run A Long Distance   Jill Baker

RUN A LONG DISTANCE

All I ask for is nothing
Everything is what I get
I never beg or borrow
What I covet I forget
Over the hills there'll be twilight
And morning hasn't broken yet

I'm a long distance runner
Ever lonely ever strange
Just a face in the maddening crowd
Nobody knows my name
Over the hills there'll be twilight
Fortune and everlasting fame

I've been in love with seven women
And I've dreamed of seven more
I'm always looking to get even
And one day settle the score
Over the hills there'll be twilight

True love and nothing more

All the pony dreams in Vegas
And the Vanderbilts of Amsterdam
Couldn't pave my path with glory
So I call my missus ma'am
Over the hills there'll be twilight
Sherwood far from Nottingham

Every bit of Sunday
Should be for Sunday things
I took a walk through the garden
And was accused of loitering
Over the hill there'll be twilight
Two mules and a daisy chain

Down in the well there's a tiger
With an oaken bucket filled with tears
You can only draw from the well
The strength of all your fears
Over the hills there'll be twilight
Whiskey in the atmosphere
The painted landscape of sorrow
Is always rendered as mud
Brother can you spare a shovel
Seven days after the flood
Over the hills there'll be twilight
And there will be blood

What our fathers said was true
Stay away from dangerous things
But our fathers played with danger
Because danger is a street thing

Over the hills there'll be twilight
Through a shady grove of reckoning

See the world properly
If you see the world at all
There are millions of miles to run
Twenty-nine million ways to fall
Over the hills there'll be twilight
Shuffling through the curtain call

Run a long distance
Down a highway in disrepair
Take care of what you carry
Mystery unravels near
Over the hills there'll be twilight
The runner disappears

HORSE RIVER BLUES

I don't walk funny
this is one long fall
I never walk funny
This is all one long fall
Every crooked step I take
is one more foot away from the law

Make the watcr wheel roll
while the baby shakes and cries
Make that water wheel roll
while the baby shakes and cries
Fewer things in this world worse
than a young girl's lies

She left me no choice
and that the choice I took
She left me no choice
which is the choice I took

Just one sinful deed to
make me a lifetime crook

Alone on the road it's cash
that's always king
When alone on the road cash
is always king
If you borrow from a shylock
it's more than a money thing

Horse River has the rapids
angels are on the shore
Horse River has many rapids
sweet angels on the far shore
If a man can cross that river
He has troubles no more

A twanging sawtooth
is nipping at my heels
That twanging sawtooth
is ripping up my heels
It's a shame to know
what real pain reveals
Goliath had a few drinks
just before David threw
Old Goliath had a few drinks
just before David threw
He had no idea
what he was getting into

I feel like Goliath and I
know that David is near

Feel just like Goliath and
fear that David is near
One more round and
boys I'm out of here

DIRTY ROTTEN DOCTOR
BLUES

I got a dirty rotten doctor
with a dirty rotten attitude
My dirty rotten doctor
has a dirty rotten attitude
Won't fix me of my pain
even though I beg him to

Said to my doctor
Man I'm in so much pain
Please my doctor
Man I'm in so much pain
He said I'll send you to the drug store
but only to buy a cane

Said I hurt so bad
doctor I can hardly walk
Said I hurt so bad
swear I can barely walk

He said I'll cure you of your limp
saw both your two legs off

Can you please my doctor
write me my two days off
Please my doctor
give me my two days off
He said I would if I could
but you might get your Ya Ya's off

My mean mad doctor
left e with the duty nurse
That mean mad doctor
left me with the duty nurse
She looked like a Viking
make you scream and curse

Gonna shoot my doctor
shoot him with a BB gun
Gonna shoot my doctor
shoot him with a BB gun
he'll know what pain is
after I get done
I got a brand new doctor
surely gonna cure my ills
My brand new doctor
surely gonna cure my ills
That kind country doctor
gave me my walking pills

Feel like 'lectricity
is loose in my spine

Feel just like 'lectricity
is loose in my spine
Don't mind me I stay
loose all the time

THE JUKE AND THE JIVE

I've lost more friends than I ever kept
Some were loners and one was a schlep
You can worry me once or worry me not
If I don't owe you money you may have a shot
At times my quarrel is with those I trust
The door is there to use if you must
I'm playing dead to get out of this alive
Shadow boxing to the rhythm of the
Juke and the jive.

The result of too much honesty can be despair
Like being in a fight with your knuckles bare
You can pivot to the left maybe shuffle to the right
Long as you keep your peripheral sight
The sweet science of humility can be so cruel
All according to the golden rule
You can get odds up to one in five
If your gibber meets the measure of the
Juke and the jive

Truth can be strange in multitude
Step away from the crowd if it bothers you
Pack all your things in a pony car
If you have the nerve to travel far
Highway sixty-one has the feel of youth
spin your wheels in the fertile root
You may by chance one day arrive
If you're jazzed to the jabbing of the
Juke and the jive

Some people are ordinary until they are rude
You have to adjust to changing attitudes
They are mean in the morning unpleasant when it's nice
You can't sell them anything at a reasonable price
They belong in line with their heart's content
Busting elbows with the rabble to save a few cents
It would not be wise to upset their hive
Let them deal with the dealing of the
Juke and the jive
You can be cheated, charged and pursued
Like a knot in an argument of no use
If you can't stand the saddle the horse is no good
Leave you in the middle of a piney wood
The stables are open for a fee
If you have the scrabble a rebel would need
It's Hobson's Choice number nine sixty-five
A nag you can ride to the
Juke and the jive

Significant women like charms on a chain
Not important how they are arranged
They shine silver and jingle like gold
Stays with a man until after he is old

Some are generous others take what they can
Tender mercies right to the bitter end
Significant women all shining live
Can make knuckles knock nimble with a
Juke and the jive

I'm guilty of everything I've ever done
I'll gladly cop to nearly one in Zen
Put me on trial for my doppelganger's tricks
I'll be happy to be rid of the sorry goldbrick
There is a shovel in my trunk that may be of use
If you have an axe and a pick and a noose
Everybody has an identity they would like to hide
Who is down for the count from the
Juke and the jive

I stepped into the ring at the prison farm
With the intent to inflict the maximum harm
A raven on the ropes was calling my bluff
Didn't think I had quite the right stuff
I've been punch drunk, solid and sour
I had no doubt I was the man of the hour
Raven said, "Throw your best shot or take a dive."
My stance was the dance of the
Juke and the jive

THE SWEETHEART PARADE

If you're playing Texas Hold-em
you may have a chance
Under a harvest moon
at The Sadie Hawkins Dance
Take that vital first step
and make your tip-toe play
By this tine tomorrow
it will be another day

(Chorus:)
When they're running out of town
make it look like a parade
With all the lovely ladies
singing your praise
And the Sheriff and the Deputies
all look the other way
It's the regular combination
The Sweetheart Parade

If you rely on liquid courage
you best fire your bartender
Never drink in public
I've been thoroughly assured
A steady hand is best played
when the odds even the numbers
Peace will have its lease
way off in the future

(Repeat Chorus)

If you know how girls talk
you're half way there
Always offer a glance
never a stare
Take her hand and lead her
when she wants to go there
By this time tomorrow
you won't have a care

(Repeat Chorus)

Courthouse Appaloosa   Jill Baker

THE COURTHOUSE APPALOOSA

I walked across the painted desert
looking to bum a ride
All my footsteps seem to gather
until they coincide
I can see the vultures circling
and there is nowhere to hide
seems like a mirage
along the Continental Divide

Calamity Jane and Annie Oakley
were at the church by noon
There was a gun fight in the street
and it couldn't happen too soon
They were singing "My Darling Clementine"
it seemed the proper tune
The undertaker bid his time
down at the Aces and Eight Saloon

Jessy James and Cole Younger

John Wesley and old Wild Bill
One was saying to the other
I'll meet you on Boot Hill
Dillinger said, "Baby Face
only kills for the thrill,"
Bonnie said to Clyde,
"Honey, just be still"

I rode the Courthouse Appaloosa
to the scene of the crime
Sam Spade was gathering clues
Agatha Christie was at the chalk outline
Sydney Greenstreet and Peter Lorre
were doing a pantomime
Louis Carroll and Edgar Allen
were talking back forth in rhyme

BLUES FOR A SILVER ROSE

Blues for a silver rose
just how the garden grows
The weeds are ineffectual
the Ivy has potential
For my blue silver rose
Blues for a silver rose
all planted in a row
The sunflower is a keeper
the willow a weeper
Like my blue silver rose

Blues for a silver rose
whenever perfect light flows
The shade seems to whisper
the blossoms say come hither
Here's to my blue silver rose

Blues for a silver rose

on anight where Venus shows
the honeysuckle and daffodil
and the lilies of the field
Love my blue silver rose

JOHN WILKES BOOTH

John Wilkes Booth, John Wilkes Booth
He spoke mind as the gospel truth
The actor of the stage with great renown
Going to kill the king and steal his crown

Like Caesar crossing the Rubicon
All bets are off and the deal ain't done
The Sons of the South will rise and win
Lee will return to Arlington

His ankle broken, his horse gone lame
Can't cross the river for the driving rain
They called him a coward, how could it be
Sic Simper Tyrannis for liberty

They don't know my mind or my plan
How can they not see they are being damned
The North has no respect for our southern ways
They burned Atlanta and worse in the coming days

He was cold and wet, hungry, on the run
His co-stars in murder all caught but one
Driven to a bar knowing the end was near
The heat of fire his greatest fear

He told his last friend, "Surrender to the devil
I'll fight to my last the curse of evil
Go now your fate is sealed;
They hang you by noon nothing is concealed

Alone in despair smoke making hi blind
He was shot by John Corbett in the nick of time
In a stranger's yard losing his senses
His last two words, "Useless, useless."

The Doomsday Switch   Jill Baker

THE DOOMSDAY SWITCH

I'm mindful of the Doomsday Switch
But it don't bother me any more
I only want to feel just
Like I did before
Thirty years is a long tine to
Keep something so neutral
Someone asks if I want their body
I say no, something more cerebral

I could join a country club
If they'd let me in
But I wouldn't want to associate with
Anyone who would treat me as kin
Ninety percent of success is
Showing up on time
All there is after that is
Surviving the punch line

Doomsday is a holiday

At the County Fair
Everybody meeting one another
A gathering of pairs
I'm on the Ferris Wheel
And I seem so all alone
This must be what it feels like
To be permanently stoned

My friends can't remember
What I can't seem to forget
Memory is a tricky thing
They haven't figured it out just yet
Sometimes it's all there
Other times it's really gone
I want to put my painting in a box
And mark it all wrong

A driving jackhammer is
Tearing up the scene
Rearranging the wallpaper
Or so it seems
There's no curtain to fall and
The pasta is always al dente
How I love the pleasures
of a wanton lazy day

I'm ever mindful of the switch
    That it is an earth device
    So what could it matter
  If it gets thrown twice
  There is relief in the courts

                    .   .   .

BUT ITS NOT THE LAW OF THE LAND
    And justice for all
    Is never written by man
    Children and Christmas Eve
    Easter in the spring
    If you work hard enough
    They can't take away anything
    All I ever wanted was
    A pretty girl all to myself
    Where is the pleasure in living
    If you can't please someone else

DON'T BOTHER TO DREAM
    It does no good
    All you can do is
    Stand where your father stood
    I might get lucky
    This may just be Mayday
    When the switch gets thrown
    And nobody notices anyway

www.ingramcontent.com/pod-product-compliance
Lightning Source LLC
LaVergne TN
LVHW021401080426
835508LV00020B/2400